21st-century SCIENCE

ENERGY

Present knowledge • Future trends

Written by Chris Oxlade

W

FRANKLIN WATTS
LONDON • SYDNEY

This edition 2007

First published in 2004 by Franklin Watts

Copyright © Franklin Watts 2004

Franklin Watts
338 Euston Road
London NW1 3BH

Franklin Watts Australia
Level 17/207 Kent Street
Sydney NSW 2000

All rights reserved.

A CIP catalogue record for this book
is available from the British Library.

Dewey number 531'.6

ISBN 978 0 7496 7378 9

Printed in China

Franklin Watts is a division of Hachette
Children's Books.

Design Billin Design Solutions
Editor in Chief John C. Miles
Art Director Jonathan Hair
Picture research Diana Morris

Picture credits
Sean Aidan/Eye Ubiquitous: 19b
Bob Battersby/Eye Ubiquitous: 10t
Andrew J.G. Bell/Eye Ubiquitous: 11b
Martin Bond/SPL: 31t, 32t
Andrew Brown/Ecoscene: 34b
Dorothy Burrows/Eye Ubiquitous: 27t
David Cummings/Eye Ubiquitous: back endpapers,
13t, 45.
Adam Hart-Davis/SPL: 36c
James Davis Worldwide: front cover bl,28b
Pat Groves/Ecoscene: front cover br
Chinch Gryniewicz/Ecoscene: 34c, 35c
Peter Hulme/Ecoscene: 6-7, 24
Graham Kitching/Ecoscene: front cover c, back cover
background, 4-5, 8
Earl & Nazima Kowall/Corbis: 17t
Genevieve Leaper/Ecoscene: 25br
Larry Lee Photography/Corbis: 40c
Keiran Murray/Ecoscene: 12c
NASA: 23, 30b, 37b
Kenvin Nicol/Eye Ubiquitous: front cover top
Novosti/SPL: 21t
H. Rogers/Eye Ubiquitous: 18c
Sandia National Laboratories/SPL: front cover bc, 20b
Alan Schein Photography/Corbis: 16b
Peter Da Silva/Corbis: 14bl.
Paul Thompson/Eye Ubiquitous: front endpapers, 39
Mark J. Tweedie/Ecoscene/Corbis: 9c
US Dept of Energy/SPL: 29t
John Wilkinson/Ecoscene: 33b
Roger Wood/Corbis: 41b
Ian Yates/Eye Ubiquitous: 26b

*Every attempt has been made to clear copyright. Should
there be any inadvertent omission, please apply to the
publisher for rectification.*

Contents

OUR NEED FOR ENERGY

Any scientist will tell you that nothing happens without energy. But what is energy? Where does it come from and how do we use it? The world needs enormous amounts of energy. Meeting these needs without further damaging the environment is one of the most serious problems we face today.

Think carefully through all the things you do in an average day. As soon as you switch on a light or a radio in the morning you start using energy. More energy is needed to heat your home, to heat water for your wash and to cool your fridge. Travelling to school by car uses more energy. So does using your computer and your mobile phone. Industry uses huge amounts of energy to process raw materials, to make them into the objects you use during the day.

Energy in the past

People have been using energy for thousands of years. At first energy was needed for heating and cooking. Later it was needed for firing pots and for smelting metals to make weapons. Most of this energy came from burning wood and plant and animal oils. Then 2,000 years ago people started harnessing the power of running water and wind to work mills for grinding corn.

Energy was first needed on a large scale in the Industrial Revolution, when coal provided heat to work steam engines. Our need for energy has risen dramatically in the last 250 years. It went up by four times in the 20th century alone as towns and cities expanded, the world became industrialised and people began to travel for work and holidays.

Towards the end of the 20th century scientists began to investigate links between our use of energy and damage to the environment.

Energy in the 21st century

Population growth (the world's population is predicted to be 9 billion by 2050) and economic development mean that our need for energy will continue to grow in the 21st century – and more quickly than it has ever grown before. Scientists and engineers need to find and develop new sources of energy to meet this demand. At the same time we need to use energy more efficiently and reduce the effects of energy use on the environment.

▲

Industrial processes, such as the metal smelting shown here, need large amounts of energy.

◄ ◄

Modern cities also require huge amounts of energy – and our needs keep growing.

ENERGY AND ENERGY CHANGES

It is not easy to define the word energy. The scientific definition is that energy is the ability to do work. For scientists, work is moving something against a force. A simple example would be lifting a bag of heavy shopping against the force of gravity. You need energy to lift the bag. In this case the energy comes from your body.

Forms of energy

Energy can take many different forms. Here are some that appear in this book.

Heat energy (also called thermal energy) is the energy an object has because of its temperature. The hotter an object is, the more heat energy it has. Adding heat energy makes an object hotter; removing heat energy makes it cooler. Don't confuse heat and temperature. For example, a red-hot spark from a fire has a much higher temperature than a mug of hot tea, but much less heat energy.

Electricity is a form of energy. An electric current is made up of tiny particles called electrons flowing along a conductor (such as a copper wire). The electrons carry electrical energy.

Light is a form of energy in the shape of electromagnetic waves. Light carries energy from place to place.

Chemical energy is the energy in a substance that can be released if the substance takes part in a chemical reaction. For example, natural gas contains chemical energy that is released when it burns. Chemical energy is a form of stored energy (or potential energy).

Kinetic energy (or movement energy) is the energy that an object has because it is moving. The faster an object is moving and the heavier it is, the more kinetic energy it has.

Changing energy

Energy can change from one form to another. For example, an electric motor turns electrical energy into kinetic energy, and a solar cell turns light energy into electrical energy. Energy changes like this are happening around us all the time.

The law of conservation of energy

Energy cannot be made and it cannot be destroyed. This fundamental law of physics means that we can't make energy, so all the energy we use must come from somewhere. It also means that when energy changes from one form to another, no energy is lost or gained, even though sometimes it seems to be.

Measuring energy and power

Energy is measured in units called joules (J). A joule is not very much energy. You use about 1,500 joules (or 1.5 kilojoules (kJ)) just walking up a flight of stairs. Power is measured in watts (W) which show how quickly energy changes from one form to another. One watt is equal to one joule per second. For example, a 100-watt light bulb changes 100 joules of electrical energy to light energy and heat energy every second.

◀ ◀

The huge speakers at this pop concert demonstrate the conversion of electrical energy into sound energy.

▼

This car on this roller coaster possesses kinetic energy, or the energy of motion.

SOURCES of ENERGY

The law of conservation of energy tells us that we can't make energy. So all the energy we need to light our homes, power our cars, work our machines and so on, must come from somewhere. We get it from the materials we find on Earth and from the environment. We can divide these energy sources into two main groups – fossil fuels and renewable sources.

Fossil fuels

Oil, gas and coal are found in the rocks of the Earth's crust. They are called fossil fuels because they are formed from the fossilised remains of plants and animals that lived millions of years ago. The energy in fossil fuels is chemical energy. We burn them to release the energy as heat and light. These ancient plants grew using energy from the Sun. The animals grew by eating plants and other animals. So the energy in fossil fuels originally came from the Sun.

In most countries between two-thirds and three-quarters of energy

comes from fossil fuels. Fossil fuels are described as non-renewable fuels because they cannot be replaced after we use them. When fossil fuels run out, we will have to get all our energy from other sources.

Renewable energy sources

'Renewables' are energy sources that are renewed after we use them. The main renewables are hydropower, wind energy, solar energy, tidal energy and bioenergy. These energy sources will never run out because they are always renewed naturally. For example, if we burn the wood from a tree to make heat, we can grow a new tree in its place. All this renewable energy starts out as heat and light from the Sun. Geothermal energy, which comes from hot rocks deep under the ground, can also be thought of as a renewable energy because of the almost limitless amount of heat inside the Earth.

Non-renewable nuclear energy

Nuclear energy is energy stored in the nuclei of atoms. It is released when a nucleus is split. Nuclear fuels come from the rocks of the Earth's crust. Although nuclear fuels are non-renewable, they release such a huge amount of energy that the energy stored in them is almost limitless.

▲

The Sun is a major source of renewable energy.

◀ ◀

Oil and gas are extracted from rocks under the seabed. All fossil fuels are non-renewable sources of energy.

ELECTRICITY SUPPLY

Electricity is an extremely convenient form of energy. It is sent to homes, offices and factories along cables, where it is easily turned into other forms of energy such as light, heat and kinetic energy. The demand for electricity is rising faster than the overall demand for energy.

The science of electricity

Devices such as electric motors, electric light bulbs and bar heaters work when an electric current flows through them. An electric current is made up of tiny particles called electrons, each of which carries a tiny electrical charge. Electrons can only move through materials called conductors, but a conductor always slows the movement of the electrons slightly. This effect is called resistance. Electrical currents only flow when an electrical force (called an electromotive force or voltage) pushes the electrons.

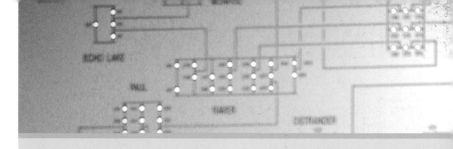

DC and AC

An electric current can be either a direct current (DC) or an alternating current (AC). A direct current flows the same way along a conductor all the time. An alternating current flows one way then the other, changing direction many times a second. An alternating current has the advantage that a device called a transformer can change its voltage.

Mains supplies

The electricity that comes from sockets in our homes (and works the lights) is called mains electricity. The electricity is made at electricity generating stations and is distributed through a grid of cables as alternating current. Homes and offices use mains electricity at voltages of 110 or 220 volts. Factories use mains electricity at much higher voltages (33,000 or 11,000 volts). This provides more power for large machinery.

Batteries

A battery is a store of energy. Inside a battery are chemicals that retain energy. When an electric circuit is connected to a battery, the chemical energy is turned into electrical energy and current flows around the circuit.

Electricity generation and distribution

Here's how electricity is generated at a generating station powered by fossil fuels and how it gets to your home.

1 Fuel is burnt, turning chemical energy present in the fuel into heat energy.

2 The heat boils water, making high-pressure steam.

3 The steam flows through turbines, making them spin.

4 Devices called generators produce electricity. A generator is a machine that turns the kinetic energy of the turbines into electrical energy.

5 The voltage is increased to hundreds of thousands of volts; transmission lines carry the electricity around the country. The high voltage reduces the amount of heat created by the resistance of the lines.

6 The voltage is decreased at a local sub-station, from where the electricity travels along wires to your home.

◄◄

Technicians monitor the distribution of electricity supplies at a control centre in California.

Fossil FUELS

At the beginning of the 21st century we are completely reliant on fossil fuels (coal, oil and gas) for our energy. In a typical economically developed country about 70 per cent of electricity is generated using fossil fuels. And cars, lorries and buses all use fuels derived from fossil fuel.

Forming fossil fuels

Coal is a solid material formed from dead plants that grew in ancient swampy forests. It is found in layers called seams, with layers of rock above and below.

Oil and gas formed from dead animals and plants that sank to the seabed and were covered by mud. As the oil and gas formed, they floated up through porous rocks (rocks with tiny holes in them) but were trapped by impermeable (non-porous rocks) forming reservoirs of oil and gas.

Finding fossil fuels

Geologists find deposits of fossil fuels by looking for patterns of rocks underground. Experience tells them which patterns are likely to yield coal, oil and gas. Geologists have many tools at their disposal. They carry out geological surveys of surface rocks, seismic surveys (sending shock waves into the ground and listening for the echoes from different layers of rocks) and look for tiny changes in the Earth's magnetic field. If rocks look likely to hold a deposit a borehole is drilled into them. If the deposit proves to be large enough, a mine is dug or an oil or gas production platform is built.

Refining crude oil

Oil that comes from the ground is called crude oil or petroleum. It is a mixture of many chemicals called hydrocarbons, which are made up mainly of the elements hydrogen and carbon. The mixture is divided up at an oil refinery. Fuels refined from crude oil include the gases butane and propane and the liquids petrol, diesel, kerosene and fuel oil. Thicker liquids from the refinery can be 'cracked' chemically to make more petrol or diesel.

Energy from fossil fuels

We have to burn fossil fuels to get the chemical energy stored in them. The energy is released as heat. Burning is a chemical reaction between the fuel and oxygen in the air. The reaction produces water vapour and carbon dioxide gases as well as heat. Liquid and solid fuels burn much faster if they are broken into tiny droplets or particles and mixed with air.

Oil shale

Oil shale is a type of rock that contains organic matter (dead animal and plant remains). If the material is heated, it turns into a fuel similar to petrol. At the moment processing oil shale (mining it, crushing it, transporting it, heating it and disposing of the waste rock) uses huge amounts of energy, but oil shale could be an important energy source in the future.

▲

Oil refineries, like this one in Singapore, process crude oil into many different products such as petrol.

◄ ◄

A massive ocean-going oil tanker loads its cargo from huge storage tanks at a refinery in North Carolina, USA.

Fossil fuel PROBLEMS

Fossil fuels are non-renewable. If we keep burning them as quickly as we are today, it is estimated that oil will run out in about 40 years' time, gas in about 70 years' time and coal in about 160 years' time. While we continue to use fossil fuels, they create pollution and other environmental problems.

The worst environmental damage is caused by emissions from power stations and engines.

Acid in the air

The elements sulphur and nitrogen are always found in coal and fuels refined from crude oil. They are difficult to remove completely. When these fuels burn, the sulphur and nitrogen combine with oxygen to form sulphur dioxide and nitrogen dioxide. These gases dissolve in the tiny drops of water that make up clouds, forming rain that is slightly acidic. When this acid rain falls it gradually makes groundwater, lakes and rivers acidic, killing trees and aquatic life.

Particulates

Particulates are tiny bits of solid matter in the air, less than a tenth of a millimetre across. Burning fossil fuels creates particulates such as smoke particles, especially if the fuels don't have enough oxygen to burn properly. As well as making the environment dirty, particulates cause breathing problems for asthma sufferers and can create smog.

Carbon dioxide and global warming

The Earth's atmosphere traps heat from the Sun because it lets heat in but stops it escaping. This is called the greenhouse effect and it helps keep the atmosphere warm.

One of the main gases causing the greenhouse effect is carbon dioxide. Carbon dioxide is always made when fossil fuels burn, and this is increasing the level of the gas in the atmosphere. Many scientists think this is trapping more heat than before. The average temperature of the atmosphere rose by 0.5°C over the 20th century and is estimated to rise another 3° C in the 21st century. This could lead to world climate change.

Pollution reduction

We can reduce acid rainfall and slow down global warming by removing the chemicals that cause them either before or after fuels are burnt. Most sulphur is removed from diesel fuel at the refinery to make low-sulphur diesel that helps to reduce acid rain.

A catalytic converter in a car's exhaust changes polluting chemicals into non-polluting chemicals (such as nitrogen dioxide into nitrogen and oxygen). Sulphur dioxide can be removed from power station emissions by devices called scrubbers. In future carbon dioxide scrubbers could remove carbon dioxide from emissions.

◄ ◄

Emissions from car exhausts contribute significantly to environmental damage.

▼

This picture shows the blanket of smog that can form over a city as a result of pollution by particulates.

NUCLEAR ENERGY

Nuclear energy is the energy stored in the nucleus of an atom. It is released as heat when a nucleus splits apart (called nuclear fission) or when two nuclei fuse together (called nuclear fusion). These events are called nuclear reactions. We use nuclear energy for generating electricity, for propelling nuclear submarines, to make electricity in space probes and to power the destructive explosions in nuclear weapons.

Nuclear fission

The nucleus of an atom is made up of particles called neutrons and protons. When a nucleus is unstable, it can split into two smaller nuclei and spare neutrons. This process is called fission. The mass of the products of fission is a tiny bit smaller than the mass of the original nucleus. This lost mass is changed into energy. A tiny amount of mass is changed into a staggering amount of energy. Just one gram of mass is equivalent to 90 million million joules – enough energy to keep a light bulb going for 30,000 years. A kilogram of uranium fuel produces as much energy as 5,000 tonnes of coal.

Nuclear reactors

At a nuclear power station, the heat from nuclear reactions is used to boil water, producing steam that drives electricity generators. The nuclear reactions happen inside a nuclear reactor. The nuclear fuel (uranium or plutonium) is contained in fuel rods, which are grouped together in the reactor's core.

About 16 per cent of the world's electricity is generated at more than 440 nuclear power stations. France generates 78.5 per cent of its electricity from nuclear energy.

Chain reaction

Many nuclear power plants use a type of uranium called uranium 235 (U235). U235 is a fissile material, which means that its atoms will split apart when it is struck by a neutron. In a nuclear reactor, neutrons are fired into the uranium fuel to split the atoms. As each atom splits it releases two or three more neutrons. They shoot off and hit other U235 atoms, splitting them and releasing even more neutrons. This chain reaction can create continuous energy.

Nuclear pros and cons

Generating electricity from nuclear energy has advantages. It does not produce acid gases or particulates and there is enough uranium in the Earth's crust to last for thousands of years. Nuclear energy's two main problems are the safe transport and storage of deadly radioactive waste from power stations and the danger of accidents, such as the 1986 explosion at Chernobyl in the Ukraine that released radioactivity into the Earth's atmosphere.

▲

An aerial view of the remains of the Chernobyl power station after the 1986 accident.

◄ ◄

Nuclear fuel rods in the core of a reactor. Disposing of spent nuclear fuel remains a huge problem.

NUCLEAR FUSION

Nuclear fusion is the opposite of nuclear fission. In a fusion reaction, two atomic nuclei are slammed together, releasing huge amounts of energy. Nuclear fusion could provide us with almost limitless energy, cleanly and safely, long into the future. But there are problems for researchers to overcome before energy from fusion comes into our homes.

Fusing nuclei

In a fusion reaction two light nuclei are fused together to form a larger, heavier nucleus. As in nuclear fission, the total mass of the products of the reaction is slightly less than the mass of the reacting nuclei and the lost mass is changed into energy.

To make fusion happen, the atoms in the fuel must be stripped of their electrons, forming a substance called plasma, made up of nuclei and electrons. Then two nuclei must be slammed into each other at incredible speed. To get the nuclei moving fast enough, they must be heated to about 100 million° C. This temperature is even hotter than the centre of the Sun and is difficult to achieve.

Fusion research

Scientists have made fusion happen in the laboratory in two ways. The first is by heating a small pellet of fuel suddenly with powerful lasers. This creates immense pressure and temperature in the centre of the pellet for a tiny fraction of a second.

The second way is in a doughnut-shaped chamber called a tokamak. A small amount of vaporised fuel is put in the container and powerful electric currents heat it to turn it into plasma. If the plasma touched the side of the container it would cool and also melt the container, so it is held away from the sides with strong magnetic fields. Although fusion reactions have happened in experimental tokamaks, at the moment the electrical energy needed to heat the plasma and work the electromagnets is greater than the energy generated inside.

Advantages of fusion

If fusion reactors become a reality, they will use two forms of hydrogen – deuterium and tritium – as fuels. These do not occur naturally, but could be made from hydrogen and lithium, which are both abundant elements in the Earth. The greatest advantage over nuclear fission is that there would be no radioactive nuclear waste to dispose of.

A fusion reaction

Deuterium and tritium are forms of hydrogen. Deuterium has one extra neutron and tritium has two extra neutrons. A fusion reaction happens when two nuclei, one from a deuterium atom and one from a tritium atom, collide at high speed. The nuclei combine to form a helium nucleus, leaving one neutron spare, and heat energy.

▲

The Sun produces unimaginable amounts of heat and light by nuclear fusion.

ENERGY from the WIND

Wind energy comes ultimately from the Sun. The Sun's rays heat the tropics more than the poles. This sets up air currents that try to spread this heat evenly over the Earth. We can use wind energy to operate machinery and to generate electricity.

Catching the wind

Wind is simply moving air, and moving air has kinetic energy. We capture this energy with windmills and wind turbines. People have built windmills for hundreds of years to operate mills for grinding wheat and to pump water from wetlands. Windmills have simple flat sails or slats, which are not very good at capturing the wind's kinetic energy. Modern wind turbines are more efficient. A wind turbine has a rotor that is turned by the wind. A turbine turns the kinetic energy in the wind into kinetic energy in the rotor. The energy from the rotor then turns a generator to produce electricity.

Turbine design

Most wind turbines have a rotor with two or three blades at the top of a tower. These are known as horizontal-axis turbines. High at the top of the tower the turbine is spun by air that flows smoothly, not by turbulent winds next to the ground.

Each blade of the turbine works like an aeroplane wing. Air flowing over a blade creates low pressure on one side, making the rotor turn. The blades have a twisted shape because the tips move faster through the air than the roots. The rotor drives a gearbox that turns an electricity generator. The rotor and generator are mounted on a rotating head, electronically controlled to keep it facing into the wind.

The world's biggest wind turbine stands 186 metres (610 feet) tall, has rotors 114 metres (375 feet) in diameter and can produce enough electricity to supply a small town.

Wind farms

For large-scale electricity production wind turbines are grouped together in 'wind farms'. A large wind farm produces about 200 megawatts of electricity – as much as a small coal-fired power station. Wind farms are sited in places where the average wind is strong and constant, such as on hilltops and along coasts.

Small-scale wind energy

Small wind turbines are useful in areas where there is no mains electricity. They provide electricity directly or recharge batteries. They are often linked with a diesel generator that starts up automatically when the wind stops blowing.

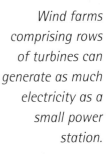

Wind farms comprising rows of turbines can generate as much electricity as a small power station.

This small wind turbine in Scotland produces enough power for a farmer's electric fence.

ENERGY from the GROUND

No matter where you are on the Earth's surface, if you dig a few thousand metres down into the ground you find hot rocks. The whole of the inside of the Earth is incredibly hot. The amount of heat energy stored here is so enormous that we can think of it as being infinite. Geothermal energy is the energy we get from this source. It is clean and renewable.

Geothermal sources

Geothermal energy comes from both hot rocks and hot underground water and steam. At the moment we use geothermal energy from sources close to the surface. These are in the volcanically active parts of the world such as New Zealand, Iceland and western USA. We use geothermal energy in two ways – 'direct use' and electricity generation.

Direct-use energy

Direct use means using hot water from deep underground and from hot springs on the surface. The most common use is for heating buildings, where the hot water is pumped through radiators. Whole towns can be heated like this. Direct-use hot water is also pumped to greenhouses where it helps plants to grow in cold climates, and to fish farms to warm the water. In the USA some pavements are kept ice-free by geothermal hot water piped under them. Geothermal water is pumped back into the ground after use to keep the underground sources topped up.

Geothermal electricity

Water that flows deep into hot rocks is heated to above boiling point, producing high pressure steam underground. The steam can be released through pipes and fed to turbines that drive electricity generators. The steam is then condensed back to water and pumped back into the ground.

◀

A geothermal power station near Taupo, North Island, New Zealand.

Geothermal heat pumps

In most places on Earth the ground just a few metres down stays at an almost constant temperature (between 10°C and 16°C) all year round, no matter what the temperature of the air is above. In winter this ground can be used as a source of energy for heating buildings. In summer the same ground can be used as a 'heat sink' to cool the same building. The technology used is called a geothermal heat pump.

Geothermal future

Research is continuing into reducing the costs of producing geothermal energy, and finding ways of using it in parts of the world that are not volcanically active. This could be achieved by boring holes up to five kilometres (three miles) deep into the Earth's crust and pumping down water to capture the heat.

◀ ◀

Hot springs can be used for bathing as well as power. This view shows the Blue Lagoon on the Reykjanes Peninsula in Iceland.

ENERGY from the SUN

Solar energy is energy we get directly from the Sun's radiation, which is made up of light and heat. In one second the Sun gives out as much energy as we use on Earth in a million years. With the Sun overhead and a clear sky, one square kilometre of ground receives enough solar energy to heat and light a small town. We can capture this energy with solar heaters and solar cells.

Solar heaters

The simplest solar heaters are made up of black panels with pipes embedded inside. The panel absorbs heat and light and warms up. The heat is transferred to air or water circulating in the pipes. In sunny countries, solar heaters are excellent for providing domestic hot water.

Electricity from heat

A concentrating solar energy system collects the Sun's rays and uses the heat to generate electricity. There are two main designs – power towers and trough collectors.

A power tower system has a central tower surrounded by hundreds of mirrors on the ground. The mirrors reflect the Sun's rays, concentrating them on to a single spot on the tower. These rays heat a liquid inside the tower which in turn heats water to make steam and drive electricity-generating turbines.

A trough collector is like a half pipe with a mirrored inside surface. It focuses the Sun's rays into a line running down its centre. Along this line is a pipe full of oil that carries the collected heat away to make steam for the turbines.

Solar cells

A solar cell (also known as a photovoltaic cell) converts light energy directly into electricity. A solar cell has two layers of semiconductor material, one above the other. When light hits the boundary between the layers it releases electrons. This creates voltage between the layers, making the cell work like a battery. A single solar cell is not very powerful, so cells are grouped together to make solar modules and arrays. Solar cells have a wide range of applications, from powering watches and calculators to running space stations.

Solar cells are not very efficient. A typical cell converts only 15 per cent of the light that hits it into electricity, and solar cells covering the area of 500 football pitches would be needed to produce as much power as a small coal-fired power station. This would be hugely expensive. However, cheaper, more efficient solar cells are being developed, based on plastics rather than semiconductors.

▲

A solar trough collector in California uses energy from the Sun – in this case to treat drinking water supplies.

◄◄

This roof-top solar-powered heater provides hot water for a house in Greece.

HYDROPOWER

Hydropower is energy from flowing water. Because most hydropower is used to generate electricity, it is also called hydroelectric power. Hydropower is a renewable energy source because water flows down rivers as part of the natural water cycle. Hydropower is one of the oldest and most widely used renewable energies, and hydroelectric power stations have been operating for more than a hundred years.

Hydroelectric power stations

At a hydroelectric power station water flows through turbines, making them spin. The turbines turn generators that make electricity. The turbines and generators convert the kinetic energy in the flowing water into electricity. There are different types of hydroelectric power stations. Most common is the impoundment station, which has a dam built across the river so that water collects behind it, forming a reservoir. The dam allows water to be released into the turbines all year round even though the river flow might go up and down.

A run-of-river (or diversion) station, the turbine sits in the flowing river water. A pump-storage station has two reservoirs; one is higher than the other. When demand for electricity is high (for example, in the early evening) water is released from the top reservoir to drive the turbines. When demand falls, spare electricity from other sources is used to pump the water from the bottom reservoir to the top reservoir.

Big dams

All major hydroelectric power stations are impoundment stations. There are several massive dams around the world that provide water to hydroelectric power stations. Some also help to control dangerous floodwaters and supply water for drinking and irrigation. A typical example is the Itaipú Dam between Brazil and Paraguay. Its eighteen turbines produce 12,600 megawatts of electricity – enough for 25 per cent of Brazil's electricity needs and 75 per cent of Paraguay's.

Hydropower problems

Hydropower may seem to be the perfect renewable energy, and many countries are building big dams to exploit the energy in their rivers. Unfortunately large dams create environmental problems. They change the pattern of river flows, blocking floods and stopping silt from being carried downstream to riverside fields. New reservoirs force people and animals from their homes. Fish and other animals are injured and killed as they pass through the turbines. These problems have led to some large dams in the USA being de-commissioned and to research into fish-friendly turbines. There is considerable opposition to new large dam projects from environmentalists.

▲

The turbine hall of a modern hydropower station in France.

◄ ◄

Hydropower is not without its problems. The delta of the River Nile in Egypt is shrinking due to dams further upstream.

ENERGY from the OCEANS

The world's oceans are a potential source of huge amounts of energy. Ocean energy comes in several different forms. There is kinetic energy in tides, ocean currents and waves, and heat energy in the warm surface waters.

Energy from the tides

The gravity of the Moon makes water move about in the oceans and the sea rise and fall at the coasts. Tidal power stations use this movement to make hydroelectricity. A tidal power station is made up of a dam across a river estuary, called a barrage, with turbines built into it. As the tide rises, water flows through the turbines into the estuary. As it falls, water flows back through the turbines to the sea. Electricity is generated when the turbines rotate in either direction. Tidal power is the only form of ocean energy currently producing electricity commercially. There are also plans to build turbines on the seabed in places where there are strong tidal currents.

Wave energy

It's estimated that the waves that hit two kilometres of coastline have as much energy as is produced by a small coal-fired power station. Researchers are investigating different ways of capturing this energy. Currently there are three different systems – floats, columns and surge systems. Floats sit in the water and bob up and down as waves pass. This movement is used to pump oil that works a turbine to produce electricity. Oscillating columns are full of air. Waves push water in and out of the column's base, which pushes air in and out of the column's top. The moving air drives a turbine. Wave surge systems collect water from the tops of the waves and let it flow back to the sea, operating a turbine on the way.

Ocean thermal energy

Oceans cover two-thirds of the Earth's surface. The Sun heats them every day, warming the surface layer. So the oceans act as a huge store of energy, known as ocean thermal energy. In the tropics the surface water can reach 25°C. Water this warm could be used to generate electricity (see explanation below). Experimental ocean thermal-energy stations have already been tested.

◄ ◄

This barrage on the River Rance in France uses the rise and fall of the tides to generate electricity.

◄

The power of waves crashing on the shore represents a huge possible future source of renewable energy.

A closed–cycle ocean thermal–energy system

In this system ammonia is heated to its boiling point by warm surface water. The pressure created by the gas formed is used to drive a turbine. Then the gas is cooled by cold water from deep in the ocean, turning it back into liquid.

ENERGY from PLANTS

Bioenergy is energy we get from plant matter such as wood. It is stored in the plants as chemical energy. The plant matter is known as biomass. Currently we use biomass for heating, generating electricity and making fuels for vehicles. Wood is the most common source of bioenergy.

Biogas digester pipes and valves in a household system.

People have burnt wood for thousands of years, with the result that many of the world's ancient forests have been destroyed. Modern bioenergy is renewable because we grow plants to replace the ones we use. Although burning biomass releases carbon dioxide into the atmosphere, the replacement plants absorb this as they grow.

Biomass sources

Almost any plant matter can be used as a biomass source, from wood and leaves to cardboard (which is made from wood pulp). Some biomass is made up of waste material from forestry (such as wood chippings), agriculture (such as straw), industry (such as paper) and animal waste. Some is from plants grown specifically for energy, known as dedicated energy crops or bioenergy feedstocks. These include fast-growing grasses such as bamboo and fast-growing trees such as willows. In the future, genetically modified (GM) crops may produce biomass faster.

Burning biomass

Some biomass is burnt as fuel to release its energy. It can be burnt alone instead of fossil fuels in electricity generating stations, and in future will be burnt (or co-fired) with coal in advanced furnaces. Some timber mills and papermaking plants burn the waste wood they produce (such as sawdust and wood chips) to produce electricity and heat.

Biomass fuels

Biomass is also converted into liquid fuels and gaseous fuels called biofuels, such as ethanol, biodiesel, hydrogen and methane. Fermenting sugars from biomass sources, such as corn and sugar cane, make ethanol. The process is similar to brewing. Researchers are looking at ways of making ethanol from plant fibres as well as sugars. Biodiesel is made from vegetable oils and waste cooking oils.

Both ethanol and biodiesel can be used alone or mixed with petrol or diesel to reduce emissions. In Brazil ethanol fermented from sugar cane makes up one-quarter of the fuel used in vehicles. Heating biomass to high temperatures without air makes hydrogen and methane. This is called gasification. Methane is also made when biomass decays naturally. Hydrogen and methane can be burnt in gas turbines or furnaces to generate electricity.

▲

A trailer is loaded with biogas from fermentation pits in Kassel, Germany.

◄ ◄

This picture shows willow shrubs being grown in Somerset to provide raw material for biogas production.

Hydrogen and fuel cells

Hydrogen is the simplest element in the universe – a hydrogen atom is made up of just one proton and one electron. Hydrogen is an excellent fuel. It can be burned to produce heat or fed into a device called a fuel cell to produce electricity. In both cases the only by-product is water, which makes hydrogen a very clean fuel.

Hydrogen is not an energy source because energy is needed to make it. But some experts think it will provide a way of storing and distributing energy in the future.

Sources of hydrogen

Hydrogen is one of the most abundant elements on Earth, but it is always locked away in other chemicals. We have to get the hydrogen out before we can use it. Our biggest sources of hydrogen are water and hydrocarbons such as natural gas. We get hydrogen from water by electrolysis (splitting something into its component parts by passing an electric current through it) and from hydrocarbons by reforming (heating them without any oxygen). We can also get hydrogen from biomass.

Burning hydrogen

Hydrogen burns very well, producing plenty of heat. The reaction with oxygen in the air makes water. Not much hydrogen is burned at present. Its main use is in rocket motors such as those in the space

shuttle. Here it is mixed with oxygen and ignited, creating a stream of hot gas that pushes the engine upwards.

Fuel cells

A fuel cell is a device that produces electricity by combining hydrogen and oxygen. You can think of a fuel cell as being like a battery that keeps supplying electricity as long as it is supplied with hydrogen and oxygen.

A fuel cell has two electrodes separated by a material called an electrolyte. Hydrogen is fed to one electrode, where it separates into electrons and protons. The protons can go through the electrolyte to the other electrode, but the electrons cannot. Instead they leave the cell creating an electric current before going back to the other electrode. Here they combine with the protons and oxygen to form water.

Using fuel cells

Fuel cells are complex devices that use rare materials, so they are expensive to make. At the moment their use is limited. Some buildings use fuel cells to provide back-up electricity supplies. Fuel cells have also been used in spacecraft for many years. And most car manufacturers have built experimental vehicles with fuel cells that power electric motors.

◄

The space shuttle blasts into orbit using the power of hydrogen fuel.

◄ ◄

A view of a hydrogen fuel cell in Europe's first hydrogen-powered taxi, unveiled in London in 1998.

ENERGY Efficiency

Energy is a precious commodity. Every time we plug in a machine or turn on an engine we use energy. Most of this energy comes from fossil fuels, so when we use energy we use up more fossil fuels and add damaging emissions to the atmosphere. We can conserve energy by using it more efficiently.

Inefficient conversions

Most energy conversions create heat as well as the form of energy we really want. For example an incandescent light bulb (a light bulb with a metal element) only converts 10 per cent of the electricity it uses into light. The rest is turned into heat, which is lost in the air. In a car only about one-quarter of the chemical energy in the petrol is turned into kinetic energy. (You can read about what happens to the rest in the panel on the right.)

Building technology

We use energy to heat and light buildings, and also to cool them with fans and air-conditioning units. Energy-efficient buildings are designed to reduce energy use. Methods of reducing energy for heating include insulating walls and windows, and using passive solar heating, which means allowing heat into a building through large windows of special glass that stop the heat escaping again.

Large windows also reduce the amount of electricity needed for lighting. So does installing energy-efficient fluorescent light bulbs and light-emitting diodes instead of standard incandescent light bulbs. The energy used for cooling can be reduced by simple methods such as planting trees to shade buildings from the Sun.

Efficient electricity

At a coal, oil or gas power station only about one-third of the energy in the fuel is converted to electricity. The rest is lost to the atmosphere as heat. Combined heat and power (CHP) stations use the waste heat to warm homes and factories close to the power station. A typical CHP station can convert 80 per cent of its fuel energy into electricity and useful heat, whereas as a conventional power station only manages around 40 per cent. CHP stations heat about half of the buildings in Denmark and Finland and a small-scale CHP unit provides light and heat for the European Parliament in Brussels.

Energy losses in a car

Three-quarters of the energy in fuel (petrol or diesel) is wasted by a car. Most of this energy goes into the atmosphere as heat. The heat is made in the engine, by the electrics, by the brakes as they slow the car, by friction in joints and bearings, and by the tyres as they move along the road. Some energy is also turned into sound.

◄

Modern office blocks can be made energy-efficient, for example, by using special glass to allow the heat from sunlight in but not out.

Energy for the FUTURE

How will our energy needs change in the 21st century, and how will we meet them? Some things are certain. Firstly, a combination of population growth and industrialisation in developing countries will mean we will need fifty per cent more energy by 2025. Secondly, global warming will create huge problems such as sea-level rises unless we cut down carbon dioxide emissions.

New technologies

Continuing research will gradually make renewable technologies more efficient and cheaper. It may also make sources of energy such as nuclear fusion and ocean thermal energy practical. Technologies such as superconductors will also allow us to use energy more efficiently. Perhaps later in the century scientists will discover a completely new source of energy. But until clean, renewable energy can supply all our energy needs, we will be reliant on fossil fuels.

Hybrid systems will help to reduce fossil fuel use. These combine renewable energy with fossil fuel energy. For example, a house might have solar panels to produce electricity during the day and draw power from the electricity grid at night.

Using new fuels

As well as finding new forms of energy, we have to develop ways of using them. For example, power stations and vehicles will have to use non-fossil fuels, such as biomass and hydrogen. We will also have to install the infrastructure to deliver fuels such as ethanol and hydrogen to where they are needed. Existing infrastructures, such as natural gas pipelines and oil refineries, will be phased out. The cost will be massive.

Regulations and incentives

People will need to be encouraged to use energy from renewable sources. Some power companies already offer people 'green' energy at extra cost with the promise that the money will be used to develop renewable energy technologies. Regulations are in force in many countries that limit the emissions allowed from vehicles and power stations, and encourage the use of small, efficient cars and cars that run on renewable fuels. Building codes make sure that new homes and offices are energy efficient.

Hydrogen in Iceland

All Iceland's electricity is produced from hydropower and geothermal energy. Hydrogen is produced by electrolysis of water using this electricity. The hydrogen is supplied to three buses powered by fuel cells in Iceland's capital, Reykjavik. This small-scale development in Iceland is an example of clean, renewable, high-technology energy at work. This may be a glimpse into the future of energy.

◄ ◄

This view from the 1980s of queues at a petrol station demonstrates the 20th century's reliance on fossil fuels.

▼

As new forms of energy become economic, laying gas pipelines will become a task of the past.

GLOSSARY

atmosphere
The blanket of air that surrounds the Earth.

battery
A device that stores energy in chemicals and gives out electricity.

bioenergy
The energy we get from plant matter (or biomass).

chemical energy
Stored energy released by a chemical reaction, such as burning gas or coal.

climate
The pattern of weather that a place has over a long period of time.

climate change
A slow change in climate over several years.

conductor
A material that allows electricity to flow through it.

electrolysis
Splitting a substance up by passing electricity through it.

generator
A device that turns kinetic energy into electricity.

geologist
A scientist who studies rocks and fossils.

geothermal energy
The energy we get from hot rocks under the ground.

global warming
The gradual warming of the Earth's atmosphere over the last century.

hydropower
The energy we get from flowing water.

Industrial Revolution
The period in history in Britain between about 1750 and 1900 when steam engines, iron and steel, steamships, trains and factories were developed.

joule
The name for one unit of energy.

kinetic energy
The energy in a moving object.

megawatt
One million watts

non-renewable
An energy source that cannot be replaced after it has been used.

nuclear energy
The energy we get from the nuclei of atoms.

porous
A substance that lets water flow through it.

power
The rate at which energy is used.

renewable
An energy source that can be replaced after it has been used.

semiconductor
A material that can act as a conductor or an insulator.

smelting
The process of producing a metal from its ore.

solar cell
A device that turns light energy into electricity.

solar energy
The energy we get from the Sun's heat and light.

tidal energy
The energy we get from the movement of the tides.

turbine
A device that turns when air or water flows through it.

voltage
The electrical 'push' that makes a current flow.

water cycle
The natural movement of water between the oceans, the atmosphere, the land and rivers.

watt
The name for one unit of power.

wind energy
The energy we get from the blowing wind.

INDEX

These are the lists of contents for each title in *21st-Century Science:*

Energy
Our need for energy • Sources of energy • Electricity supply • Fossil fuels • Nuclear energy • Wind energy • Geothermal energy • Solar energy • Hydropower • Energy from the oceans • Biomass energy • Hydrogen and fuel cells • Energy efficiency • Energy for the future

Medicine
The living machine • Breakdowns in the body • The body under attack Fighting back • Battling bacteria • Coping with cancer • Complementary medicine • Tools of the trade • Surgery • The genetic revolution • Life in vitro • Medicine in space

Genetics
All about genetics • Chromosomes • DNA • Genes at work • Life begins • Inheriting genes • When genes go wrong • Changing DNA • Gene-splicing • Plant genetics • Mixing animal DNA • Cloning • How will we use genetics? • Genetic mysteries

Telecoms
The pace of change • Signals, senders and receivers • Wires, fibres and aerials • Multiplexing • Networks • Computer networks • Terrestrial communications • Freedom from wires • Cellular mobiles • Satellite communications • The Internet • Broadcasting • The future

Electronics
The world goes electronic • Circuits and signals • Computer building blocks • Memory • Microprocessors • CPU logic • Chip design • Making a chip • Circuit boards • Electronic sound • Displays • Sending signals • Flying electronics • The future of electronics

New materials
Raw materials • Metals • Polymers and plastics • Fibres and composites • Adhesives and superglues • Ceramics and glass • Clever crystals • Silicon • Fuels for the future • Manipulating molecules and genes • Materials in space • Conservation and recycling